First World War
and Army of Occupation
War Diary
France, Belgium and Germany

1 DIVISION
1 Infantry Brigade
Trench Mortar Battery
2 July 1917 - 31 December 1918

WO95/1266/3

The Naval & Military Press Ltd
www.nmarchive.com
Published in association with The National Archives

Published by

The Naval & Military Press Ltd

Unit 10 Ridgewood Industrial Park,

Uckfield, East Sussex,

TN22 5QE England

Tel: +44 (0) 1825 749494

www.naval-military-press.com

www.nmarchive.com

This diary has been reprinted in facsimile from the original. Any imperfections are inevitably reproduced and the quality may fall short of modern type and cartographic standards.

© **Crown Copyright**
Images reproduced by permission of The National Archives, London, England, 2015.

Contents

Document type	Place/Title	Date From	Date To
Heading	WO95/1266/3		
Heading	1st Division 1st Trench Mortar Battery July 1917 To 1918 Dec		
Heading	1st Trench Mortar Battery 1st Division July 1917		
War Diary	Newport Bains	02/07/1917	02/07/1917
War Diary	Coxyde Bains	03/07/1917	16/07/1917
War Diary	Bray Dunes Area	17/07/1917	17/07/1917
War Diary	Le Clipon	18/07/1917	31/07/1917
Heading	1st Trench Mortar Battery 1st Division August 1917		
War Diary	Le Clipon	01/08/1917	31/08/1917
Heading	1st Trench Mortar Battery 1st Division September 1917		
War Diary	Le Clipon	01/09/1917	30/09/1917
Heading	1st Trench Mortar Battery 1st Division October 1917		
War Diary	Le Clipon Camp	01/10/1917	20/10/1917
War Diary	Feggers Cappel	21/10/1917	21/10/1917
War Diary	Arneke Area	22/10/1917	25/10/1917
War Diary	Nouveau Monde Area	26/10/1917	31/10/1917
Heading	1st Trench Mortar Battery 1st Division November 1917		
War Diary	Noveau Monde Area	01/11/1917	06/11/1917
War Diary	Schools Camp	07/11/1917	08/11/1917
War Diary	Dambre Camp	09/11/1917	15/11/1917
War Diary	Irish Farm	16/11/1917	20/11/1917
War Diary	Dambre Camp	21/11/1917	22/11/1917
War Diary	Road Camp	23/11/1917	27/11/1917
War Diary	Praed Camp	28/11/1917	30/11/1917
Heading	1st Trench Mortar Battery 1st Division December 1917		
War Diary	Yser Canal Bank	01/01/1918	30/01/1918
War Diary	Noordhoek	31/01/1918	08/02/1918
War Diary	S.22.d.9.5	08/02/1918	09/02/1918
War Diary	Canal Bank	10/02/1918	20/02/1918
War Diary	Hill Top Farm	21/02/1918	04/03/1918
War Diary	Seige Camp	05/03/1918	07/03/1918
War Diary	Millain	07/03/1918	14/03/1918
War Diary	Seige Camp	15/03/1918	16/03/1918
War Diary	Caddie Camp	17/03/1918	29/03/1918
War Diary	Gournier Farm	30/03/1918	31/03/1918
Heading	1st T.M. Btty April 1918		
War Diary	Gournier Camp	01/04/1918	07/04/1918
War Diary	Mortar Camp	08/04/1918	08/04/1918
War Diary	Marles Les Mines	09/04/1918	11/04/1918
War Diary	Houchin	12/04/1918	12/04/1918
War Diary	Fouquerueil	13/04/1918	16/04/1918
War Diary	Givenchy	18/04/1918	22/04/1918
War Diary	Houchin	23/04/1918	23/04/1918
War Diary	Noeux Les Mines	24/04/1918	02/05/1918
War Diary	Cambrin	20/05/1918	20/05/1918
War Diary	Noeux Les Mines	20/05/1918	28/05/1918
War Diary	Battery Headquarters Cannon Street G 3 D.15.60	01/06/1918	13/06/1918
War Diary	Braquemont Camp	14/06/1918	21/06/1918
War Diary	Headquarters Wimpole Street A26 B.6.7	21/06/1918	21/06/1918

War Diary	Wimpole St Cambrin	01/07/1918	11/07/1918
War Diary	Noeux Les Mines	11/07/1918	20/07/1918
War Diary	Noeux Les Mines	21/07/1918	21/07/1918
War Diary	Cannon Street	21/07/1918	31/07/1918
War Diary	Hohenzollern Sector	01/08/1918	10/08/1918
War Diary	Noeux Les Mines	10/08/1918	19/08/1918
War Diary	Quevaussart	20/08/1918	20/08/1918
War Diary	Fontaine Les Boulons	20/08/1918	31/08/1918
War Diary	Arras	01/09/1918	02/09/1918
War Diary	Achicourt	05/09/1918	05/09/1918
War Diary	Arras	06/09/1918	08/09/1918
War Diary	Etrun	10/09/1918	10/09/1918
War Diary	Morcourt	11/09/1918	12/09/1918
War Diary	Tertry	13/09/1918	13/09/1918
War Diary	Caulincourt	14/09/1918	14/09/1918
War Diary	Marteville (Ref. Sheet 62 B)	17/09/1918	24/09/1918
War Diary	Vermand	26/09/1918	30/09/1918
War Diary	M 11 B Foreats Trench	01/10/1918	04/10/1918
War Diary	Vermand	09/10/1918	09/10/1918
War Diary	Onoto Trench G.28a	16/10/1918	16/10/1918
War Diary	Bohain	17/10/1918	17/10/1918
War Diary	Vaux Andigny	18/10/1918	18/10/1918
War Diary	La Vallee Mulatre	20/10/1918	22/10/1918
War Diary	Wassigny	23/10/1918	27/10/1918
War Diary	La Vallee Mulatre	01/11/1918	03/11/1918
War Diary	Mazinghiem	04/11/1918	04/11/1918
War Diary	Vaux Andigny	05/11/1918	05/11/1918
War Diary	Fresnoy-Le-Grand	06/11/1918	12/11/1918
War Diary	Grand Fayt	13/11/1918	14/11/1918
War Diary	Sars Poteries	15/11/1918	15/11/1918
War Diary	Hestrad	16/11/1918	16/11/1918
War Diary	Castillon	18/11/1918	18/11/1918
War Diary	Laneffe	19/11/1918	22/11/1918
War Diary	Stave	23/11/1918	23/11/1918
War Diary	Weillen	24/11/1918	01/12/1918
War Diary	Veve	02/12/1918	02/12/1918
War Diary	Mt Gauthier	03/12/1918	07/12/1918
War Diary	Haversin	08/12/1918	09/12/1918
War Diary	Saillionville Barurox	10/12/1918	10/12/1918
War Diary	Bomal	11/12/1918	13/12/1918
War Diary	Grand Menil	14/12/1918	14/12/1918
War Diary	Petites Tailles	15/12/1918	15/12/1918
War Diary	Cierreux	16/12/1918	16/12/1918
War Diary	Thommen	17/12/1918	17/12/1918
War Diary	Amelacheld	18/12/1918	18/12/1918
War Diary	Hallschlag	19/12/1918	19/12/1918
War Diary	Schmidtheim	20/12/1918	21/12/1918
War Diary	Manstereifel	22/12/1918	22/12/1918
War Diary	Kuchewheim	23/12/1918	23/12/1918
War Diary	Bornheim	24/12/1918	31/12/1918

WO 95/1266/3

1ST DIVISION

1ST TRENCH MORTAR BATTERY
~~JUL - DEC 1917~~

July 1917 to 15/18 Dec

1st TRENCH MORTAR BATTERY

1st DIVISION

JULY   1917

WAR DIARY

INTELLIGENCE SUMMARY
(Erase heading not required.)

1st Trench Mortar Battery
For month of July 1917

Army Form C. 2118

Instructions regarding War Diaries and Intelligence Summaries are contained in F.S. Regs., Part II. and the Staff Manual respectively. Title Pages will be prepared in manuscript.

Place	Date 1917	Hour	Summary of Events and Information	Remarks and references to Appendices
Nieuport Bains	2nd July		Bombarded enemy trenches for 20 minutes, firing 600 rounds, prior to a raid made by a party of the 1st Battalion. The Black Watch	S/101
Coxyde Bains	3rd July		Relieved by 3rd Trench Mortar Battery and moved to BADOR camp, in reserve	S/101
"	4th July to 11th July		Training	S/101
Bray Dunes area	12th July		Moved to BRAY DUNES area	S/101
Le Clipon	15th July		Moved to LE CLIPON camp	S/101
"	16th July to 31st July		Training	S/101

Strangeways Edwards Capt.
1st Trench Mortar Battery

1ST TRENCH MORTAR BATTERY

1st DIVISION

AUGUST 1917

Army Form C. 2118

WAR DIARY

1st Trench Mortar Battery

(Erase heading not required.)

Instructions regarding War Diaries and Intelligence Summaries are contained in F. S. Regs., Part II. and the Staff Manual respectively. Title Pages will be prepared in manuscript.

Place	Date	Hour	Summary of Events and Information	Remarks and references to Appendices
Re Alyon	1/6/17 to 2/6/17		Training	

Strangus Glenoche Capt.
1st Trench Mortar Battery

1ST TRENCH MORTAR BATTERY

1st DIVISION

SEPTEMBER 1917

Army Form C. 2118

WAR DIARY
INTELLIGENCE SUMMARY
(Erase heading not required.)

Instructions regarding War Diaries and Intelligence Summaries are contained in F.S. Regs., Part II. and the Staff Manual respectively. Title Pages will be prepared in manuscript.

Place	Date	Hour	Summary of Events and Information	Remarks and references to Appendices
Le Clipon	1.9.17 to 30.9.17		Training	

Montague Wheeler Capt.
1st French Mortar Battery

1875 Wt. W593/826 1,000,000 4/15 J.B.C. & A. A.D.S.S./Forms/C. 2118.

1st TRENCH MORTAR BATTERY

1st DIVISION

OCTOBER 1917

Army Form C. 2118.

WAR DIARY
or
INTELLIGENCE SUMMARY.
(Erase heading not required.)

Instructions regarding War Diaries and Intelligence Summaries are contained in F. S. Regs., Part II. and the Staff Manual respectively. Title pages will be prepared in manuscript.

Place	Date	Hour	Summary of Events and Information	Remarks and references to Appendices
Le Meleure Camp	1.10.17 to 19.10.17		Training	
Zeggers-Kappel	20.10.17		Moved to Zeggers Kappel	
Vlamke area	21.10.17		Moved to Vlamke area	
	22.10.17		Training	
	23.10.17		"	
	25.10.17		"	
Nouveau Monde area	26.10.17		Moved to Nouveau Monde area	
	27.10.17		Training	
	31.10.17		"	

Ivor Mackintosh Lieut.
O.C. 1st T.M.B.

1st TRENCH MORTAR BATTERY

1st DIVISION

NOVEMBER 1917

1st Trench Mortar Battery

WAR DIARY for month of November 1917

Army Form C. 2118.

INTELLIGENCE SUMMARY

(Erase heading not required.)

Instructions regarding War Diaries and Intelligence
Summaries are contained in F. S. Regs., Part II.
and the Staff Manual respectively. Title pages
will be prepared in manuscript.

Place	Date	Hour	Summary of Events and Information	Remarks and references to Appendices
Moreau Circle Area	1.11.17 to 5.11.17		Training SMB	
	6.11.17		Moved to SCHOOLS Camp SMB	
Schools Camp	7.11.17		Training SMB	
	8.11.17		Moved to DAMBRE Camp SMB	
Dambre Camp	9.11.17 to 14.11.17		Training SMB	
	15.11.17		Moved into Reserve at IRISH FARM. SMB	
Irish Farm	16.11.17		Fatigues SMB	
	17.11.17		Moved to DAMBRE Camp SMB	
Dambre Camp	21.11.17		Training SMB	
	22.11.17		Moved to ROAD Camp SMB	
Road Camp	23.11.17 to 26.11.17		Training SMB	
	27.11.17		Moved to PRAED Camp SMB	

1st Trench Mortar Battery.

Army Form C. 2118.

WAR DIARY for month of November 1917 (continued)
INTELLIGENCE SUMMARY.
(Erase heading not required.)

Instructions regarding War Diaries and Intelligence Summaries are contained in F. S. Regs., Part II. and the Staff Manual respectively. Title pages will be prepared in manuscript.

Place	Date	Hour	Summary of Events and Information	Remarks and references to Appendices
Grand Camp	1st to 11/17 to 6 30.11.17		Training	
			J. Montague Glendler Capt. O.C. 1st T.M.B.	

1st TRENCH MORTAR BATTERY

1st DIVISION

DECEMBER 1917

1st Trench Mortar Battery

WAR DIARY for month of January, 1918

INTELLIGENCE SUMMARY.

(Erase heading not required.)

Army Form C. 2118.

Instructions regarding War Diaries and Intelligence Summaries are contained in F. S. Regs., Part II. and the Staff Manual respectively. Title pages will be prepared in manuscript.

Place	Date	Hour	Summary of Events and Information	Remarks and references to Appendices
YSER CANAL BANK	1-1-18 to 29-1-18		Repairing and maintaining DELAHOUSSE Track from CANAL BANK to the CORPS WIRE. Repairing and maintaining HERBEBOIS Track from DELAHOUSSE Track to the BROENBEEK.	Shelled Shelled Shelled Shelled
	30-1-18		Moved to NOORDHOEK to billets at S.22.d.9.5 - map sheet 20.	
NOORDHOEK	31-1-18		Cleaning Billets. R.BERKS section rejoined unit.	

Stradacquit Clericke Capt.
1st T.M.B.

1st Trench Mortar Battery for month of February 1918. Army Form C. 2118.

WAR DIARY
or
INTELLIGENCE SUMMARY.
(Erase heading not required.)

Place	Date	Hour	Summary of Events and Information	Remarks and references to Appendices
NOORDHOEK	1/2/18 to 8/2/18		Training	MS
S.22.d.9.5			10th Gloucesters Section joins Unit.	MS
"	4/2/18		Moved to CANAL BANK. C 25.d.	MS
	9/2/18		1st Loyal North Lancs. Section reports for duty.	MS
CANAL BANK	10/2/18			
"	10/2/18 to 19/2/18		Training	MS
	20/2/18		Moved to HILL TOP FARM. Relieved 2nd Bde Brigade in line, occupying defensive position	MS
HILL TOP FARM	20/2/18 to 23/2/18		Training and improving Emplacements in line. Making new emplacements Rear Sections. Salvaging.	MS

L. Moekitt Lieut.
1st T. M. Battery.

SECRET

1st Trench Mortar Battery

WAR DIARY for month of March 1918. Army Form C. 2118.

INTELLIGENCE SUMMARY.

(Erase heading not required.)

Instructions regarding War Diaries and Intelligence Summaries are contained in F. S. Regs., Part II. and the Staff Manual respectively. Title pages will be prepared in manuscript.

Place	Date 1918	Hour	Summary of Events and Information	Remarks and references to Appendices
HILL TOP FARM	1-3-18 to 14-3-18		Making new Emplacements in Line.	M.
"			Rear Section Salvaging.	M.
"	4-3-18		Relieved by 5th T.M.B. and took over Billets in Camp III SEIGE CAMP.	M.
SEIGE CAMP	5-3-18 to 7-3-18		Training	M.
"				M.
"	7-3-18		Proceeded by Motor to II Corps School, MILLAIN	M.
MILLAIN	7-3-18 to 13-3-18		Training	M.
MILLAIN	14-3-18		Returned by Motor to Camp III SEIGE CAMP.	M.
SEIGE CAMP	15-3-18		Training	M.
"	16-3-18		Moved from SEIGE CAMP to CADDIE CAMP. Two guns in the Line	M.
CADDIE CAMP	17-3-18 to 28-3-18		Rear Section Salvaging	M.
"	29-3-18		Moved to GOURNIER FARM.	26
GOURNIER FARM	20-3-18 to 30-3-18		Rear Section Salvaging	M.

Jas Nichol Lt
1st T.M. Battery

1st TN Bttn

April, 1918.

Army Form C. 2118.

WAR DIARY for month of April 1918.
INTELLIGENCE SUMMARY.   1st Trench Mortar Battery
(Erase heading not required.)

Instructions regarding War Diaries and Intelligence
Summaries are contained in F. S. Regs., Part II.
and the Staff Manual respectively. Title pages
will be prepared in manuscript.

Place	Date 1918	Hour	Summary of Events and Information	Remarks and references to Appendices
GOURNIER CAMP	April 1st		2 guns in line. Rear Section carrying parties.	Smy
	2nd		Rear Section carrying parties.	Smy
	3rd 4th 5th		Rear Section salvaging.	Smy
	6th			Smy
	7th		Relieved by 89th Brigade T.M.B. Moved by road to Mortar Camp Elverdinge.	Smy
MORTAR CAMP	8th		Training. Moved by road to Peselhoek. Entrained to Choques and moved	Smy
			by road to MARLES LES MINES.	Smy
MARLES LES MINES	9th 10th		Training.	Smy
MARLES LES MINES	11th		Moved by road to HOUCHIN.	Smy
HOUCHIN	12th		Moved by road to FOUQUEREUIL.	Smy
FOUQUEREUIL	13th 14th 15th		Training.	Smy
	16.		Relieved 164 T.M.B. in GIVENCHY Sector. Headquarters WESTMINSTER BRIDGE.	Smy
GIVENCHY	18	4 a.m.	German attack. 2 Officers 25 O.R. missing. 1 O.R. killed.	Smy
	22nd		Relieved by 164 T.M.B. Proceeded by motor to HOUCHIN.	Smy
HOUCHIN	23rd			Smy
	24th 25th 30th		Moved by road to NOEUX LES MINES.	Smy
NOEUX LES MINES			Training	Smy

SECRET

Army Form C. 2118.

WAR DIARY for Month of May 1918.
of
INTELLIGENCE SUMMARY. 1st Trench Mortar Battery

(Erase heading not required.)

Instructions regarding War Diaries and Intelligence Summaries are contained in F. S. Regs., Part II. and the Staff Manual respectively. Title pages will be prepared in manuscript.

Place	Date	Hour	Summary of Events and Information	Remarks and references to Appendices
NOEUX LES MINES.	1st		Training	Sh/t
"	2nd		Relieved 2nd T.M.B. in CAMBRIN SECTOR. Eight guns in line.	Sh/t
"			Headquarters WIMPOLE STREET.	Sh/t
CAMBRIN.	20th		Relieved by 3rd T.M.B. Took over Billets from 3rd T.M.B. in NOEUX LES MINES.	Sh/t
	20th/28th		Training.	Sh/t
NOEUX LES MINES	28th		Relieved 2nd T.M.B. in HOHENZOLLERN SECTOR. Eight guns in line	Sh/t
"			Headquarters G.3.a. 30.85.	

Shadayne Knight
Capt
1st T.M.B

SECRET 1st Trench Mortar Battery

WAR DIARY for month of June 1918.

INTELLIGENCE SUMMARY.

(Erase heading not required.)

Army Form C. 2118.

Instructions regarding War Diaries and Intelligence Summaries are contained in F. S. Regs., Part II. and the Staff Manual respectively. Title pages will be prepared in manuscript.

Place	Date 1918	Hour	Summary of Events and Information	Remarks and references to Appendices
BATTERY HEADQUARTERS. CANNON STREET G.3.a.15.60.	June 1/30 to 13th		Eight guns in line in HOHENZOLLERN SECTOR.	2h.
do	—13th		Relieved by 3rd T.M.B. and took over lines in BRAQUEMONT CAMP.	2h.
BRAQUEMONT CAMP.	14th to 20th		Training	2h.
BRAQUEMONT CAMP.	21st		Relieved 2nd T.M.B. in CAMBRIN SECTOR. Headquarters WIMPOLE STREET. A.26.b.6.7. Eight guns in line. Construction of new emplacements	2h. 2h.
HEADQUARTERS WIMPOLE StREET. A.26.b.6.7				2h.

La Moulin(?) Capt.
Comdg. 1st T.M. Battery

CONFIDENTIAL 1st Trench Mortar Battery WAR DIARY for month of July 1918.

Army Form C. 2118.

Instructions regarding War Diaries and Intelligence Summaries are contained in F. S. Regs., Part II. and the Staff Manual respectively. Title pages will be prepared in manuscript.

INTELLIGENCE SUMMARY.
(Erase heading not required.)

Place	Date	Hour	Summary of Events and Information	Remarks and references to Appendices
Headquarters				
WIMPOLE ST.	July 1st to 10th			9B.
CAMBRIN.		11th	8 guns in line in CAMBRIN SECTOR.	9B.
WIMPOLE ST.		11th	Relieved by 2nd T.M.B. Troops over Billets in NOEUX LES MINES.	9B.
NOEUX LES MINES		11th to 20th	Training.	9B.
NOEUX LES MINES		21st	Relieved 2nd T.M.B. in HOHENZOLLERN SECTOR. Headquarters CANNON STREET.	9B.
CANNON STREET.		21st 26 31st	6 guns in line in HOHENZOLLERN SECTOR.	9B.

Jos. Budge Lieut.
1st Trench Mortar Battery

1st Trench Mortar Bty WAR DIARY or INTELLIGENCE SUMMARY.
(Erase heading not required.)

Army Form C. 2118.

Place	Date	Hour	Summary of Events and Information	Remarks and references to Appendices
HOHENZOLLERN SECTOR.	Aug 1st to 10th		In line.	
	10th		Relieved by 3rd T.M.B. Went over Billets in NOEUX LES MINES.	
NOEUX LES MINES.	10th to 14th		Training.	
do	14th		Moved to Bivouacs near NOEUX LES MINES on account of hostile shelling.	
do	14th to 16th		Training.	
do	19th		Moved by Bus to QUEVAUSSART.	
QUEVAUSSART.	20th		Moved to FONTAINE LES BOULONS.	
FONTAINE LES BOULONS	20th to 31st		Training.	
	31st		Moved by train to ARRAS.	

Ian Mash M.
Commdg 1st I. M. Battery

CONFIDENTIAL

WAR DIARY for month of September 1918.

INTELLIGENCE SUMMARY

(Erase heading not required.)

1st Trench Mortar Battery

Army Form C. 2118.

Instructions regarding War Diaries and Intelligence Summaries are contained in F.S. Regs., Part II. and the Staff Manual respectively. Title pages will be prepared in manuscript.

Place	Date	Hour	Summary of Events and Information	Remarks and references to Appendices
ARRAS.	1918 Sept 1st		Battery Headquarters in Caves.	n
"	Sept 2.		Moved from Cave to Trench Shelters in ACHICOURT.	"
ACHICOURT.	" 5.		Moved from ACHICOURT to cellars in ARRAS.	"
ARRAS.	" 6,7,8.		In cellars in ARRAS.	"
ARRAS.	Sept 8.		Moved by road to ETRUN.	"
ETRUN.	10		Entrained at MAROEIL and detrained at MARCELCAVE. Marched to dug outs at MORCOURT.	"
MORCOURT.	11th, 12th		Salvaging.	"
MORCOURT	12th		Embussed at MORCOURT and debussed at MONTECOURT. Marched to shelters in TERTRY	"
TERTRY.	13th		Marched from TERTRY to huts near CAULINCOURT.	"
CAULINCOURT	14		Marched from CAULINCOURT to trench shelters near MARTEVILLE.	"
MARTEVILLE.	17th		No 2. Section attached to 1st Cameron Highlanders. No 3. Section attached	"
(Ref. Sheet 62B)			to 1st Loyal North Lancashire Regiment.	"
			No 1 Section Prisoner of War Guard at QUARRY R.34.a.	"
			Battery Headquarters at VERMAND.	"
	18th		Nos 2 and 3 Sections assembled with the support company of their	"
			respective Battalions.	"

WAR DIARY
or
INTELLIGENCE SUMMARY.
(Erase heading not required.)

Army Form C. 2118.

Instructions regarding War Diaries and Intelligence Summaries are contained in F.S. Regs., Part II. and the Staff Manual respectively. Title pages will be prepared in manuscript.

Place	Date	Hour	Summary of Events and Information	Remarks and references to Appendices
			Their subsequent operations were as follows:-	
	18th		No 3. Section (Supporting 1st Loyal North Lancashire Regt.) Moved forward with support Company from assembly position.	X
		6.15	"C" Company 1st Loyal North Lancashire Regt. called for Trench Mortars to come forward and deal with hostile Machine gun firing from front. Fire was opened on it and Machine gun put out of action.	X
		6.50 am	"A" Company 1st Loyal North Lancashire Regt. called for French Mortar Support against a nest of hostile Machine guns on their right flank. The mortars were brought into action with some effect but owing to number of hostile Machine guns and difficulty in locating them their fire could not be completely stopped.	X
		7.30 am	"D" Company 1st Loyal North Lancashire Regt. called for French Mortar support against a hostile Machine gun which was engaged and silenced. Mortars then took up defensive positions covering the Battalion front in case of counter attack from the front line. The Section was withdrawn at 11 p.m. the guns being out of action through Shell fire. It relieved No 1 Section of Cameron Highlanders.	X
	18		No. 2. Section (Supporting 1st Cameron Highlanders)	2

Army Form C. 2118.

WAR DIARY
or
INTELLIGENCE SUMMARY.
(Erase heading not required.)

Place	Date	Hour	Summary of Events and Information	Remarks and references to Appendices
			Moved forward with Support Company from Assembly position to the first objective, whence it advanced towards BERTHAUCOURT with leading companies. Moved up to Sunken Road in M.15.a.2.4. and located hostile Machine guns which it successfully engaged, one machine gun being just out of action, and the other forced to withdraw along a trench two allowing 'A' Company 1st Canadian Highlanders to move forward and contact the right flank. Defensive positions were then taken up at M.14.b.8.7.	
	19th		Defensive positions were changed to M.15.a.1.4 firing on LEDUC TRENCH, End of Sunken Road in M.15.a. and FOURNOY ALLEY in M.15.a. and b. Hostile Machine guns and trenches were engaged from QUARRY at M.15.a.4.6. A captured German 3" Trench Mortar was brought into action from Sunken Road at M.15.a.45.85. and engaged PONTRUET Village and PONTRUET, PALAIRE and BRIENT trenches with shrapnel and percussion. Enemy Machine guns about M.9.d.7.8. receiving special attention. Enemy machine guns firing from Valley in M.15.c. were engaged for 1st The Black Watch	
	18 to 23rd		No 1 Section Prisoner of War guard. After 12 noon 19th carrying ammunition to forward sections. Battery Headquarters at MAISSEMY at R.23.b.55.40.	
	20.21.22		No 2 Section. Engaged trench targets. On the afternoon of the 22nd this section was withdrawn into Reserve at MAISSEMY.	

WAR DIARY
or
INTELLIGENCE SUMMARY

(Erase heading not required.)

Army Form C. 2118

Place	Date	Hour	Summary of Events and Information	Remarks and references to Appendices
	Sept 20.		No 1 Section went into line to support 1st The Black Watch taking up positions in VILLEMAY TRENCH in M.20.b. and firing on ESSLING ALLEY, ARBOUSIERS WOOD and VILLEMAY TRENCH in M.21.a and c.	
			At midnight Sept 23/24 this Section was withdrawn	
	22.		No 3 Section returned to the line to support 1st Loyal North Lancashire Regt. and engaged enemy machine guns and trenches in M.9.d and M.15.a and c. It was withdrawn at 12 midnight Sept 23/24.	
	23/24 12 midnt.		Battery moved to VERMAND.	
VERMAND.	26.		Moved to VADENCOURT.	
			1 Subsection of No 3 Section supported 1st Loyal North Lancashire Regt. on the left with position in FOURMI TRENCH.	
			No 2 Section and 1 Subsection No 3 Section supported 1st The Black Watch on the right. Positions at (2 guns) M.9.c. central and (1 gun) M.9.c.3.1.	
			These guns engaged PONTRUET.	
	27.		Two right guns moved forward to PALARIC TRENCH.	
			1 Subsection of No 3 Section was withdrawn and joined 1st Loyal North Lancashire Regt.	

WAR DIARY
or
INTELLIGENCE SUMMARY

Army Form C. 2118

Place	Date	Hour	Summary of Events and Information	Remarks and references to Appendices
	Sept 29		and was replaced on right by one Subsection of No 2. Section.	
			Battery Headquarters moved to PONTRUET at M9 d 6.8.	
			No 1. Section put down a barrage in FORGANS TRENCH and advanced with 1st The Black Watch through FOREATS TRENCH taking up positions in Sunken road at M12 a 1.8.	
			No 3. Section withdrew to QUARRY at M2 b 7.4 and joined "A" company 1st Loyal North Lancashire Regt. It advanced with them to PEN TRENCH engaging enemy machine guns	
			No 2 Section withdrew to Brigade Reserve in PONTRUET.	
	30th	6 am	Battery Headquarters moved to FOREATS TRENCH in M11 b.	
		8.30 am	No 1 Section bombarded Trench at M 12 b and advanced with 1st The Black Watch taking up positions at N 8 c 2.8.	
		10 pm	No 1 Section withdrew to Battery Headquarters, FOREATS TRENCH.	

Capt.
Comdg 1st Trench Mortar Battery

CONFIDENTIAL

Army Form C. 2118.

WAR DIARY for month of October 1918.

INTELLIGENCE SUMMARY.

1st Trench Mortar Battery.

(Erase heading not required.)

Instructions regarding War Diaries and Intelligence Summaries are contained in F.S. Regs., Part II. and the Staff Manual respectively. Title pages will be prepared in manuscript.

Place	Date	Hour	Summary of Events and Information	Remarks and references to Appendices
MILL & FORESTS TRENCH	Oct 1st–3rd		Battery in Brigade Reserve.	
	4th	2 p.m.	Battery moved to Vermand in area X.1.c.	Sh. (Sheet 62c)
VERMAND	9th		Moved to ONGTO TRENCH G.28.c.	Sh. (Sheet 62c)
ONGTO TRENCH G.28.c	10th		Moved to billets in BOHAIN D.21.d.4.8. Number 2 Section into action in support of 1st American Expeditionary forces. (Sheet 62.B)	Sh. (Thorigny Sheet)
BOHAIN	17th	4 a.m.	Battery Headquarters moved to FARM at D.4.d.4.7.	Sh. (3.no 62.c)
		12.00	Battery Headquarters moved to VAUX ANDIGNY at W.20.c.7.9. Number 1 Section into action at ANGEN FARM W.22.c.6.0.	(Andigny Forest Sheet)
VAUX ANDIGNY	18		Battery Headquarters moved to LA VALLEE MULATRE. W.21.b.b.b. Number 2 Sec.	Sh.
LA VALLEE MULATRE	20		No 1 Section withdrawn from line to Battery Headquarters.	Sh.
	22		Battery moved to WASSIGNY. X.26.d.6.5. No 1 and No 2 Sections went into line in support of 2nd Infantry Brigade by putting down a barrage in support of 2nd Canadian Divisions on the 23rd.	Sh.
WASSIGNY	23		No 1 and No 2 Sections withdrawn to Battery Headquarters.	Sh.

Army Form C. 2118.

WAR DIARY
or
INTELLIGENCE SUMMARY.
(Erase heading not required.)

Instructions regarding War Diaries and Intelligence Summaries are contained in F. S. Regs., Part II. and the Staff Manual respectively. Title pages will be prepared in manuscript.

Place	Date	Hour	Summary of Events and Information	Remarks and references to Appendices
MASSINY	24		No 1 Section went into line in support of 1st Ch[..]Blackwatch	
	25		Battery Headquarters moved to R.31. No 2 Section went into Sp (above 17B.SP)	
			in support of Lyon Park Grosvenor Rd.	
	27		Whole of the Trench Mortar Howitzers and their ammn put up at VALLEE MULATRE	

_____
Captain
O.C. T.M. TRENCH MORTAR BATTERY.

Army Form C. 2118.

WAR DIARY
1st Trench Mortar Battery
or
INTELLIGENCE SUMMARY. for November 1918

(Erase heading not required)

Instructions regarding War Diaries and Intelligence Summaries are contained in F. S. Regs. Part II. and the Staff Manual respectively. Title pages will be prepared in manuscript.

Place	Date	Hour	Summary of Events and Information	Remarks and references to Appendices
La Vallée Mulatre	1-2nd		Training	X.
"	3rd	6=20-00	Sections joined the respective Battalions and proceeded to attack positions near	X.
Mazinghem	4th		the CANAL de la SAMBRE S.E. of CATILON. Battery HQs. and to MAZINGHEM Section attached and crossed the Canal with their battalions. Support to H.Q.	X.
		21-00	M.G.s	X.
			Sections were withdrawn to Battery Hqs.	X.
Vaux Andigny	5th		Battery moved to VAUX ANDIGNY to billets	X.
Fresnoy-	6th		Moved to FRESNOY-LE-GRAND, to billets	X.
le-Grand	7th			X.
	12th		Training	X.
Grand Fayt	13th		Moved to GRAND FAYT by bus	X.
	14th		Training	X.
Sars Poteries	15th		Moved to billets in SARS POTERIES by road	X.
Hestrud	16th		Moved to billets in HESTRUD	X.
Castillon	18th		Moved to billets in CASTILLON	X.
Laneffe	19th		Moved to billets in LANEFFE	X.
"	20th		Training	X.
"	22nd			X.
Stave	23rd		Moved to billets in STAVE	X.

WAR DIARY *or* ~~INTELLIGENCE SUMMARY~~

Army Form C. 2118.

1st Fld. How. Battery for Nov. 6a 1918

Place	Date	Hour	Summary of Events and Information	Remarks and references to Appendices
Weillen	24th		Moved to billets in WEILLEN	Lt. Ll.
"	25th 6.30ᵃ		Training	

Jas Macdonald

Army Form C. 2118.

WAR DIARY
or
INTELLIGENCE SUMMARY.

1st Trench Mortar Battery for December.

(Erase heading not required.)

Instructions regarding War Diaries and Intelligence Summaries are contained in F. S. Regs., Part II. and the Staff Manual respectively. Title pages will be prepared in manuscript.

Place	Date	Hour	Summary of Events and Information	Remarks and references to Appendices
WEILEN	1st		Marched to billets in VEYE by route march	
VEYE	2nd		" " " " Mount Gauthier " "	
Mt Gauthier	3rd		Staying	
"	to 6th		"	
"	7th		Marched to billets in HAVERSIN by route march	
HAVERSIN	8th		Staying	
"	9th		Marched to billets in SAILLONVILLE – BARVAUX by route march	
Saillonville, Barvaux	10th		" " " " BOMAL " " "	
BOMAL	11th		" " " " A Farm Pon BOMAL " " "	
"	12th		Staying	
"	13th		Marched to billets in GRAND MENIL by route march	
GRAND MENIL	14th		" " " " BEKKES TAILLES " " "	
Bekkes Tailles	15th		" " " " CIERREUX " " "	
CIERREUX	16th		" " " " THOMMEN " " "	
THOMMEN	17th		" " " " AMELACHEID " " "	

WAR DIARY

1st Trench Mortar Battery — Army Form C. 2118.

for December

Place	Date	Hour	Summary of Events and Information	Remarks and references to Appendices
Amelscheid	18th		Marched to billets in HALLSCHLAG	
Hallschlag	19th		" " " " SCHMIDTHEIM	
Schmidtheim	20th		Training	
"	21st		Marched to billets in MANSTEREIFEL	
Mansteresfel	22nd		" " " " KUCHENHEIM	
Kuchenheim	23rd		" " " " BORNHEIM	
Bornheim	24th to 31st		Training	

for Capt
Comdg. 1st T.M. Battery

www.ingramcontent.com/pod-product-compliance
Lightning Source LLC
Chambersburg PA
CBHW081500160426
43193CB00013B/2548